RECIPE FOR♥LIFE

FEASTING ON GOD'S GRACE

T. WESEMANN

www.CTAinc.com

Recipe for Life: Feasting on God's Grace
by T. Wesemann
www.timwesemann.com

Copyright © 2006 by CTA, Inc.
1625 Larkin Williams Rd.
Fenton, MO 63026-1205

ISBN 1-933234-08-3
Printed in Thailand

To:

You're blessed
when you've worked up
a good appetite for God.
He's food and drink
in the best meal you'll ever eat.
Matthew 5:6 THE MESSAGE

I appreciate your appetite for God!
Your life and faith
have blessed me.

I thank God for you!

From:

Date:

Your words are so choice,
so tasty;
I prefer them
to the best home cooking.
With your instruction,
I understand life.
Psalm 119:103–104 THE MESSAGE

TABLE OF CONTENTS

THE RECIPES

*W*hile God's recipe for an abundant life remains the focus of this book, every chapter includes a recipe or two for more earthly cuisine that you can use in your home or share with others. May these recipes for earthly goodies bless you, but may they be overshadowed by your hunger for God's Word as you feast on his goodness and grace!*

Thank you, CTA staff and families, for sharing your recipes!

In a well-furnished kitchen
there are not only crystal goblets
and silver platters,
but waste cans and compost buckets—
some containers used to serve fine meals,
others to take out the garbage.
Become the kind of container
God can use
to present any and every kind of gift
to his guests for their blessing.
2 Timothy 2:20–21 THE MESSAGE

You prepare a table before me
in the presence of my enemies.
Psalm 23:5

PREPARATION

SETTING
THE TABLE

"I'm hungry! Is dinner ready?"

Searching for just the right recipe, we page through *The Book* on the counter. Thumbing through its pages, we run across this recipe for a meal called *life:*

John 10:10
From the hearth
(and the heart!) of Jesus:

I came that they may have life
and have it abundantly.

Serves: Everyone!

The Book, written long ago, has passed from generation to generation. Its recipes have proven healthful and life-giving. Scrawled across the bottom of this particular page we find these words:

Variation on John 10:10:

[Jesus said,] "*I came so they can have real and eternal life,*
more and better life than they ever dreamed of."

THE MESSAGE

Real life! Eternal life! A better life than we ever dreamed of! What a recipe for life Jesus provides for us. The ingredients, the way they go together to make up the meal, and all the fixin's that add to the appeal—all are gifts from the Bread of Life himself, Jesus. He has come to give us a real, eternal, and better life than we could ever dream of. An abundant life! The perfect meal!

It says here that in the meal of *real life,* the food and drink come from the Lord. God provides not only the invitations, but also all the ingredients, the table decorations—everything! Great news! No trip to the market. No shopping for the best quality or the best bargains. Any preparation for the meal on our part grows out of amazed love and wonder at the Lord's gracious invitation to dine with him. Let the preparations begin as we head to the kitchen!

But Wait!

The recipe book says . . . *wait!* Before we move ahead, I should be honest with you and let you know that I spend a lot of time in the kitchen. I have a problem (one of many). It's a *wait* problem. I can't *wait* for the next meal! So I snack and snack and snack and now . . . I have a *weight* problem!

But that's what the recipe says, with explanation: "Wait!"

> *The eyes of all look to you, and*
> *you give them their food in due season.*
>
> *Psalm 145:15*

One of my favorite writers, Eugene Peterson, has paraphrased this verse this way:

> *All eyes are on you, expectant;*
> *you give them their meals on time.*
>
> *Psalm 145:15 THE MESSAGE*

We need not worry about anything; our Lord waits on (I mean *serves*) us! He gives us everything we need at just the right time. In fact, he models perfectly how we can serve others.

One day while I defrosted the last piece of frozen low-fat-no-taste double chocolate cake with chocolate-chip icing, I realized I wasn't the only one with a *wait* problem. These words caught my eye. They were served up, as it were, on a tray held by the psalmist, who obviously served as a *wait-er*.

I wait for the LORD, my soul waits,
and in his word I hope;
my soul waits for the Lord
more than watchmen for the morning,
more than watchmen for the morning.
O, Israel, hope in the LORD!
For with the LORD there is steadfast love,
and with him is plentiful redemption.

Psalm 130:5–7

Plentiful redemption. Now that's something I can sink my teeth into. I checked the nutritional value and found nothing harmful in this recipe, only nutrients designed to nourish my faith. In the Lord's kitchen preparation time cannot be rushed. I wait for the Lord's timing, as he works in every circumstance for my good.

The plentiful redemption the psalmist pictured is

- healthier than the freshest salad;
- sweeter than fresh corn on the cob
- juicier than tenderloin perfectly prepared;
- more filling than pasta alfredo with pesto;
- richer than a just-out-of-the-oven chocolate-chip cookie; and
- more satisfying than a cool glass of water on a hot summer's day.

Can't you just taste it now? Savor the wonderful aroma.
Oh, I can't take it anymore. Just talking about it makes
the cravings start . . .

Okay, I'm back. Please forgive the break, but I had to
have a taste.

On the Right Front Burner . . .

I found this:

> [The Lord says,] "I, even I,
> am he who blots out your transgressions,
> for my own sake, and remembers your sins no more."
>
> Isaiah 43:25 NIV

On the left front burner I found this:

> Peace I leave with you; my peace I give to you.
> Not as the world gives do I give to you.
> Let not your hearts be troubled,
> neither let them be afraid.
>
> John 14:27

And an attractive plate sitting invitingly out on the counter overflows with these tasty morsels:

Keep yourselves in God's love as you wait for the mercy of our Lord Jesus Christ to bring you to eternal life.

Jude 21 NIV

To him who is able to keep you from falling and to present you before his glorious presence without fault and with great joy—to the only God our Savior be glory, majesty, power and authority, through Jesus Christ our Lord, before all ages, now and forevermore! Amen.

Jude 24–25 NIV

Talk about filling, satisfying, and nourishing!

Now, like infants at the breast, drink deep of God's pure kindness. Then you'll grow up mature and whole in God. You've had a taste of God.

1 Peter 2:2–3 THE MESSAGE

Our Lord invites us to become connoisseurs of his grace, savoring every morsel he serves up for our growth in grace. The Father delights in serving us, his children. He finds great satisfaction in having his family gather in the kitchen of his home, feasting on all the nourishing fare he prepares for us. Our God supplies our every need according to his riches in glory in Christ Jesus (Philippians 4:19).

As the Lord serves up his recipe for an abundant life, we realize immediately the need to prepare our hearts as we stand in the presence of our God. Standing in the presence of our perfect Savior, we see our imperfections. We often ask for a *whine* list or create an inventory of excuses. Instead, our Savior calls us to repentance—a turning away from our sins as we run into his arms for forgiveness and peace. The apostle John shares with us this banquet of grace and assurance:

> *If we say we have no sin, we deceive ourselves,*
> *and the truth is not in us.*
> *If we confess our sins, he is faithful and just to forgive us*
> *our sins and to cleanse us from all unrighteousness.*
>
> 1 John 1:8–9

The Lord seasons these delicacies further with his promise to remember our sins no more (Psalm 103:12; Hebrews 8:12). Our guilt and shame disappear, replaced by confidence in the cross of Christ.

On the Refrigerator Door . . .

As we prepare our hearts to feast with our Lord, we see he has arrived in advance and made his own preparations. He even takes care of those little touches that make many kitchens the heart of the home. There, on the refrigerator, as it were, we notice a cross-shaped magnet. It holds a note written by our heavenly Father:

I love being the Giver of heavenly flavors.

I want you to learn the art of the connoisseur!

Like Ezekiel, learn to appreciate my Word—
sweet as honey.

Take and drink my pure, life-giving milk,
my kindness in Christ!

You will grow strong in faith as you feast on my food,
having tasted that I am good.

Based on Ezekiel 3:3; 1 Peter 2:2–3; Psalm 34:8–10.

"You Prepare a Table"

Our Good Shepherd prepares a table for us in the presence of our enemies (Psalm 23:5). Not until adulthood did someone explain that line of the psalm to me. Why would the Lord prepare a table for sheep? Sheep graze in fields, not on tables.

But the shepherds of David's day easily understood. The author of this psalm, the future king of Israel, David himself, often led his sheep to graze on the flat tablelands or mesas. But good shepherds knew that amidst the nutritional grass on the mesa-table, harmful weeds and other plants also grew. Before leading his sheep to eat on such a table, the chief shepherd or one of his helpers climbed the steep sides of the mesa ahead of the flock and removed all the noxious weeds and anything else that could harm the sheep. He set up salt blocks in the areas where grass was most plentiful, thus attracting the sheep away from danger. In other words, a good shepherd prepared a table for his sheep in the presence of harmful enemies.

What enemies threaten you today? Who or what endangers you as Jesus prepares a table for you? Illness? A sinful habit? Debt? Depression? The hurtful words of others? Guilt? Bitter people wanting to unleash their anger on you? Loneliness? An addiction? Death? The devil?

Knowing the care and compassion of our Good Shepherd, Jesus, we can dine in peace—a peace only our Good Shepherd can bring. Protected, we, his sheep, may safely graze while gazing into his eyes of grace.

What to Wear to the Feast

As we prepare to join the Lord at his table, we may wonder what to wear. It's laid out for us right here:

Therefore, as God's chosen people, holy and dearly loved, clothe yourselves with compassion, kindness, humility, gentleness and patience. Bear with each other and forgive whatever grievances you may have against one another. Forgive as the Lord forgave you. And over all these virtues put on love, which binds them all together in perfect unity.

Colossians 3:12–14 NIV

Dressed in this wardrobe given to us as a gift by the Holy Spirit, we approach the table in confidence and joy. Heaven's angels stand guard around the Lord's kitchen of grace. Do you notice the startlingly white tablecloth? It's cut from the same fabric as Christ's own robe of righteousness. It represents the purity of forgiveness we enjoy before the Father.

Do you see the plates, platters, and goblets from which the Holy Spirit serves us? They proclaim the flawlessness of the Potter who designed and crafted them—each unique, each created perfectly to present the Lord's lavish gifts to his dinner guests.

Do you admire the table utensils made of gold? They remind us of the Spirit-created faith and Spirit-directed Word that sustain us even through the refining fires that blaze around us.

In this you greatly rejoice, though now for a little while you may have had to suffer grief in all kinds of trials. These have come so that your faith—of greater worth than gold, which perishes even though refined by fire— may be proved genuine and may result in praise, glory and honor when Jesus Christ is revealed.

1 Peter 1:6–7 NIV

The Center-Peace

Despite these wonders, our attention turns as our Savior-Host enters the room carrying the centerpiece for the table. Seeing it, we realize a better description would be *center-peace.* Jesus places his cross in the center of our feast. One side reveals the ruggedness of this tool of execution. Three nails remain there as reminders that Christ crucified stands at the center of a life of peace. He alone makes possible a forgiven, abundant, and eternal life. Living white lilies adorn the other side of the cross. They remind us of Jesus' resurrection and the resurrection gift he gives to all who dine with him.

Have you ever feasted at a more beautiful or lavish table setting? Take a seat. Are you hungry? starved for acceptance? dying of thirst? We're almost ready to eat! You'll find God's heavenly kitchen open (along with his arms of love). And there's no charge; it's all on the house—God's house of grace.

The table is set! Taste the Lord's plentiful redemption. You'll never hunger again! Taste and see! The Lord is good!

Let's pray, and then let the feasting begin!

Make a joyful noise

to the LORD all the earth!

Serve the LORD

with gladness!
Come into his presence
with singing!

Know that the LORD

he is God!
It is he who made us,
and we are his;
we are his people,
and the sheep of his pasture.

Enter his gates
with thanksgiving,
and his courts with praise!

Give thanks to him;
bless his name!

For the LORD is good;
his steadfast love endures forever,
and his faithfulness to all
generations.

Psalm 100

Mealtime Prayers

Thank you for the world so sweet.

Thank you for the food we eat.

Thank you for the birds that sing.

Thank you, God, for everything. Amen.

Loving Father,

we thank you for this food and for all your blessings to us.

Lord Jesus, come and be our guest,

and take your place at this table.

Holy Spirit, as this food feeds our bodies, so we pray you

would nourish our souls. Amen.

RECIPE FOR LIFE

We thank you, Lord, for happy hearts,
for rain and sunny weather.
We thank you, Lord, for this food
and that we are together. Amen.

Bless us, O Lord, and these, your gifts that we are
about to receive from your bountiful goodness.
Through Christ, our Lord. Amen.

Lord Jesus Christ, as you blessed many with the five
loaves and the two fish, may we, too, know your
blessing as we share this food, your peace in our
hearts, and your love in our lives. Amen.

RECIPE FOR L

How sweet are your words to my taste.

THE PRAYER

SAYING
GRACE

With the table set, the feast will follow. Before we pray, giving thanks to God for his grace and goodness, we need to check on one thing. Is everyone seated and ready to eat, or is there a Martha on the loose in the kitchen? Sure enough! There's at least one in every kitchen! The Host speaks up, "You are agitated and upset about many things. Let me quiet you with my love and presence." (See Luke 10:38–42.)

The Marthalike figure wipes her hands on her apron. The apron reads: "*Stressed* Spelled Backwards Is *Desserts.*" She stands back to consider the mess she's made. To a fermenting, rising mound of anxiety she has added a dash of haste, more than a pinch of worry, and an overflowing cup of unsifted anger toward her sister in Christ. That sister sits, Marylike, at Jesus' feet. She wears an apron, too. But hers reads: "Too *Blessed* to Be *Stressed.*"

Our Host, Jesus, gently removes Martha's messy apron, revealing his righteousness, the righteousness that covers her beautifully from head to toe. He quiets her with his grace and forgiveness and invites her to the table to savor the real, necessary-for-life nourishment he has prepared. When all are similarly seated, the meal can begin.

"Grace!"

Even in non-Christian families, banquets like the one we are about to enjoy call for a blessing. Even unbelievers recognize the appropriateness of thanking the Feast Maker, our Creator and Provider.

But even Christian families often include a clown. When prompted, "Let's say grace," the children will often respond in a chorus of "Grace!" They mean no disrespect. Their growling stomachs and the delicious aromas rising from the table just seem to activate their silly bones.

You've been there, too, I would imagine, surrounded by a chorus of growling stomachs waiting for "grace" so you can all have your fill. But perhaps other hunger pains have surrounded you also. Perhaps you have been hungry for answers to tough questions, starved for attention, famished for relief from the pain, looking ravenously for a break from the pressure, hungry for compassion.

Grace Enough

We've all been there—the apostle Paul, too. He was hungry. But before the Lord satisfied Paul's hunger pangs, he spoke grace to Paul's heart. The apostle writes about his famous "thorn" in 2 Corinthians 12:7–9. The word *thorn* can be translated in a variety of ways. It can describe a stake used for impaling or torturing someone, a sharpened wooden staff, or simply an everyday splinter. Whatever tortured him, Paul hungered for relief, for help. The Lord knew Paul's hunger. God heard his repeated pleas. And the Lord said grace. To be precise, the Lord told Paul, "My grace is sufficient for you, for my power is made perfect in weakness."

With those words, Paul's hunger subsided. Take note of the change that followed. Paul began to delight in weaknesses, insults, hardships, and persecution. He realized that when he was weak, he was strong. The Lord gently removed the cotton that Satan had placed in Paul's ears. The Holy Spirit came close and whispered in his servant's ear, "Grace, Paul. My grace. It is sufficient!" Paul tasted that grace and trusted the truths of God's nourishing Word.

Receiving God's gift of grace, Paul learned contentment. He could relax in God's love despite his circumstances (Philippians 4:11–12). He learned to give
thanks in all situations (1 Thessalonians 5:18). He realized more fully the importance of prayer (Romans
8:26–27; Ephesians 3:16–19; 1 Thessalonians 5:17).

Hang on Tightly!

So are you hungry today? The grace God
gave Paul can satisfy your heart, too. Allow the Host at
your table to say grace. It will be sufficient.

Then hang on tightly for the ride that will surely follow! God's grace will turn your world upside down!
You might find yourself rejoicing while the rest of the
world moans. You may start loving the people whom
everyone else around you hates. You may find yourself
boasting in the Lord rather than yourself.

Hang on for the ride that follows, because giving
thanks in all circumstances will turn your world upside
down! But what a blessing to see with eyes of faith that
wrap every circumstance in thanksgiving!

Hang on for the ride that follows, because praying con-
tinually will turn your world upside down! From this

vantage point you will enjoy a new intimacy with your Savior. Listening for his answer to your prayers and watching to see how he answers them will change how you spend your time. And the more you talk with him, the easier discerning his will becomes.

Saying Grace, Showing Grace

As long as we live here on earth, our hunger pangs will sometimes flare up. We need someone to say grace. Our Lord Jesus has. From his cross he spoke a loud word of grace that echoes forever through heaven's banquet hall. His love satisfies our hunger completely. His grace is sufficient!

> *[Jesus said,] "My grace is sufficient for you,*
> *for my power is made perfect in weakness."*
>
> *2 Corinthians 12:9*

> *Give thanks to the LORD, for he is good;*
> *his love endures forever.*
>
> *Psalm 107:1 NIV*

Therefore,
as you received
Christ Jesus the Lord,
so walk in him,
rooted and built up in him
and established in the faith,
just as you were taught,
abounding in thanksgiving.
Colossians 2:6–7

You shall love
the LORD your God
with all your heart
and with all your soul
and with all your might.
Deuteronomy 6:5

You're blessed
when you've worked up
a good appetite for God.
He's food and drink in the best meal
you'll ever eat.
Matthew 5:6 THE MESSAGE

The Spirit of God
whets our appetite
by giving us a taste
of what's ahead.
He puts a little of heaven
in our hearts
so that we'll never settle for less.
2 Corinthians 5:5 THE MESSAGE

Cheesecake Fruit Dip

8 ounces cream cheese
½ cup margarine
¾ cup powdered sugar
1 tablespoon brown sugar
2 teaspoons vanilla
Dash of allspice

Soften cream cheese and margarine.
Mix all ingredients until smooth. Enjoy!

RECIPE FOR LIFE
How sweet are your words to my taste. Psalm 119:

Hot Crab Spread (yields 2 cups)

8 ounces cream cheese, softened
1 tablespoon milk
2 teaspoons Worcestershire sauce
1 6-ounce can king crab, drained and flaked
2 tablespoons chopped green onions
2 tablespoons toasted slivered almonds

Preheat oven to 350º.
Combine cream cheese, milk, Worcestershire sauce,
crab, and green onions. Place in small
individual casseroles. Sprinkle with
almonds. Bake uncovered at 350º for
15 minutes. Serve hot with assorted crackers.

RECIPE FOR LIFE
How sweet are your words to my taste. Psalm 119:103

Sausage Biscuit Bites

Preheat oven to 400°.

Crumble and cook 1 pound bulk sausage; drain.

Mix 1 pound shredded sharp cheddar into the sausage, until the cheese melts. Stir in 3 cups of Bisquick® until smooth. Chill about 30 minutes.

Shape into small balls and place on ungreased baking sheet. Bake 8–10 minutes. Drain on paper towels. Serve warm.

(Note: These store well in an airtight container or can be frozen. Reheat in a slow oven.)

RECIPE FOR LIFE
How sweet are your words to my taste. Psalm 11

Appetizer Recipes

APPETIZERS

FIRST THINGS
FIRST

Dictionary.com defines an appetizer as "a food or drink served usually before a meal to stimulate the appetite." Great chefs intend appetizers to whet our appetites for more. But too often I fill up on appetizers, leaving little room for the main course!

On summer vacation in Tuscany, my family and I enjoyed a unique eating experience at a restaurant that looked more like an Italian home. No flashing signs announced its location; in fact, I don't recall seeing any signs outside the building. (I guess only those "in the know" knew about it, and I'm not sure how we ended up there!) The waiter/host, who also served as one of the two chefs and likely owned the restaurant, seated us at an outdoor table under a beautiful summer Tuscan sky. Because neither the servers nor the chefs presented menus, we selected only our drinks and ate what they brought us. Every dish, from the appetizers to dessert, was made with ingredients handpicked fresh that day.

But that wasn't all! A tempting variety of appetizers truly did whet our appetites for the next course! Since our feast lasted almost six hours, and since we didn't know when the next course would be served, we had plenty of time to grow our appetites. Dinner Tuscany-style comes with a "No Rushing" clause.

So while we grew our appetites, we talked and visited, catching up on the events of the day. We enjoyed the beautiful fields of sunflowers that surrounded us. And we continued visiting, planning upcoming side trips. (Did I mention that we enjoyed the beautiful fields of sunflowers that surrounded us?)

Whenever the servers brought the next course, we were ready, hungry again because we had taken our time as we savored each and every course, allowing each taste of the paradiselike fare to whet our appetites for the next. Each course drew *oohs* and *ahhs*. Two to three hours passed before the main course arrived—a variety of seafood taken from the water just hours before.

That evening the appetizers lived up to their definition as "food or drink served . . . to stimulate the appetite." No doubt about it, the savory appetizers more than whetted my appetite for the next course, and the next course always arrived at just the right time.

Fast Food, Anyone?

We live in a fast-food society—and I'm not referring to the chains of restaurants that sit on every corner. We eat as quickly as we rush through the rest of our day. We rush to get ready in the morning so we can sit in rush-hour traffic. We zap a quick breakfast in the microwave, hoping it will add some zip to our day. The notes in our day planners spill over into the margins. Twenty-four hours never seem to be quite enough. We rush through our times of private devotions, failing perhaps most days to take the time to savor the Savior's love.

But right now, as our divine Host serves an appetizer, let's allow the definition of the word to ring true: "a food or drink served usually before a meal to stimulate the appetite." Our Lord wants us to enjoy larger appetites—for him, his Word, and his ways.

The Spirit of God whets our appetite
by giving us a taste of what's ahead.
He puts a little of heaven in our hearts so that
we'll never settle for less.
2 Corinthians 5:5 THE MESSAGE

How beautiful! How true! Daily the Holy Spirit desires to whet our appetites so we hunger more deeply for the feast God prepares for us. Constantly the Spirit desires to stimulate our appetites for more of the real life, the abundant life, that Jesus won for us on his cross. But so often we power walk to the next appointment on our schedule, missing out on so much of the true power God wants to give us.

Still, the Spirit continues to put the taste of heaven in our hearts, so that we will never contentedly settle for less. Our God serves up a slice of heaven so we will slow down and . . .

- receive his full and free forgiveness;
- experience his peace, the peace that surpasses all human understanding;
- gather with Christian friends to enjoy their love and grow stronger through their witness;
- find joy in giving and serving;
- discover the pleasure of giving thanks in all circumstances;
- fully trust him and his promises—no matter the situation—with the faith the Holy Spirit creates in us;
- listen—truly listen—for his answer to our prayers;
- forgive and love others as we have been forgiven and loved by Christ;
- hurt with the wounded and give thanks with those rejoicing; and
- seek first the kingdom of God and his righteousness (Matthew 6:33).

How's Your Appetite?

Do you hunger for a larger taste of heaven on earth? Do you long for the feast of heaven itself? Having tasted the life that culminates in heaven, we might think we'd never settle for less.

But we do, don't we? We try to satisfy our hunger by filling our lives with things that amount to spiritual junk food. What are your life priorities right this minute? Go ahead. Try this task.

NUMBER THE FOLLOWING, ASSIGNING THE NUMBER **1**
TO YOUR HIGHEST-PRIORITY ITEM AND **10**
TO YOUR LOWEST PRIORITY.

___ Relationships/Friendships   ___ Finances

___ Job   ___ Family life/
                                         Family relationships

___ Appearance
                                    ___ Worship/Church

___ God
                                    ___ Volunteering

___ Recreation/Pleasure
                                    ___ Material things

If you're like me, thinking about life priorities makes you feel as though your travel agent booked you on a sudden guilt trip. You may want to make God your number-one priority, but deep down you know how often you've failed to put him first.

Stop Right There!

I confess. I posed a trick question.

You've just thought about a misleading survey. There's more to the story of "[seeking] first the kingdom of God and his righteousness" as Jesus has commanded. Our God, our Lord and Savior, wants to be involved in every single aspect of our lives! Think about it this way:

- Jesus wants to walk with us into all our relationships, causing them to flourish.
- Jesus desires to work alongside us.
- Jesus hopes we will include him in decisions about our appearance.
- Jesus requests to serve as Chief Financial Officer of our home.
- Jesus loves joining our families in everything we do (and also as we relax deeply, doing nothing).

- Jesus wants to be the focus of our worship and of all our works of service.
- Jesus can give us his wisdom in making decisions about every aspect of the material things that surround us.

In other words, Jesus is first when he is a part of every aspect of our lives, every relationship we cherish. And as we include him, we . . .

- keep first things first;
- seek first the kingdom of God and his righteousness;
- allow the Spirit of God to whet our appetite for what's ahead, putting a little taste of heaven in our hearts so we'll never settle for less; and
- discover the grace that brings the abundant and eternal life our Lord has planned for us.

Now fear the LORD
and serve him with all faithfulness.
Throw away the gods
your forefathers worshiped
beyond the River and in Egypt,
and serve the LORD.
But if serving the LORD
seems undesirable to you,
then choose for yourselves this day
whom you will serve,
whether the gods your forefathers
served beyond the River,
or the gods of the Amorites,
in whose land you are living.
But as for me and my household,
we will serve the LORD.

Joshua 24:14–15 NIV

Oh, taste and see that
the LORD is good!
Blessed is the man
who takes refuge in him!
Psalm 34:8

You did not choose me,
but I chose you and appointed you
to go and bear fruit—
fruit that will last.
John 15:16 NIV

Romaine and Broccoli Salad

Toss together:

    1 head romaine lettuce
    1 bunch broccoli (or cauliflower), chopped into bite-size pieces
    4 scallions, chopped

        Sauté in 4 teaspoons of butter:

            1 cup chopped walnuts (or pecans)
            1 package Ramen noodles, crumbled
            Oriental seasoning packet from Ramen noodles package

RECIPE FOR LIFE ♥

How sweet are your words to my taste.   Psalm 119:103 NLT

Chicken Chili

2 teaspoons olive oil
1 large onion, chopped
3 cloves garlic
1 pound boneless chicken, chopped into
    half-inch pieces
¼ cup chili powder

2 15-ounce cans black beans, drained
2 15-ounce cans chopped tomatoes
15-ounce can tomato sauce
1½ cups frozen corn
Green peppers, chopped
½ cup cilantro leaves

    Brown onion, garlic, and chicken in olive oil. Transfer
    to a large soup pot and add remaining ingredients.
    Simmer for 1–2 hours or until vegetables and chicken
    are cooked through.

RECIPE FOR LIFE ♥

How sweet are your words to my taste.   Psalm 119:103 NLT

(Romaine and Broccoli Salad, continued)

Cool and drain on paper towels.

Mix dressing by whisking together:
- ⅓ cup oil
- ¼ cup red wine vinegar
- ¼ cup sugar
- 1½ teaspoon soy sauce
- Salt and pepper to taste

Toss all ingredients with the dressing.

Tortellini Soup

1 12-ounce package tortellini
4 14½-ounce cans chicken broth
1 medium onion
4 stalks celery, chopped
4 carrots, chopped
2 chicken bouillon cubes

Cook vegetables in broth until tender. Add bouillon cubes. Cook tortellini as directed, drain. Add tortellini to soup. Add salt and pepper to taste.

RECIPE FOR LIFE
How sweet are your words to my taste. Psalm 119:10

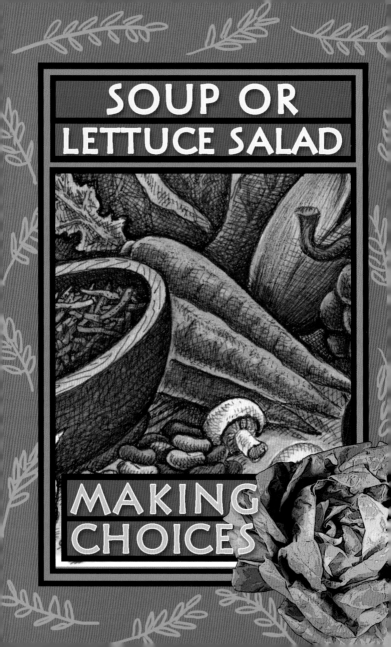

SOUP OR
LETTUCE SALAD

MAKING
CHOICES

Decisions, decisions! If you love making choices, you will enjoy dining at a restaurant where choices come served up faster than the food. Think about it:

- Smoking or nonsmoking?
- Table or booth?
- Lemon or no lemon in your water?
- Regular or diet cola?
- Small, medium, or large?
- Menu, soup and salad bar, or tonight's special?
- Soup or side salad?
- What kind of dressing?
- What two sides would you like?
- What kind of beans—green beans, lima beans, baked beans, black beans, white beans, kidney beans, lentil beans, fava beans, pinto beans, or soybeans? (What's that? You changed your mind? You want spinach instead?)
- Rolls, corn bread, biscuits, white bread, wheat bread, rye bread?
- Salt or pepper?
- And now for your dessert choices . . .

Ahhhhhh! Decisions, decisions! We make a wide range of choices every day—from the seemingly insignificant to the life altering.

- Should I turn right here, or will that be wrong?
- Should I wear red or white today, and if I wear red *and* white will I feel blue?
- Should I fix fish for dinner or just fish something microwavable out of the freezer?
- Should I buy generic diapers or pamper my baby and spend a little more?
- Should I attend the late service at church and arrive early or arrive late at the early service?
- Should I chaperone the dance or dance around commitment?
- Should I retire and move south, or am I just tired having realized most of my body has already moved south?

Choices Consistent with Abundant Life

Are you one who makes decisions easily, or do you abhor making any decision? If you can't decide how to answer that question, you probably fall into the latter category!

When it comes to making choices in the recipe for an abundant life that Christ offers, consider these tasty thoughts . . .

1. We acknowledge that what we might consider an insignificant choice isn't insignificant to God. If it matters to us, we can be assured it matters to him. And even when it doesn't matter to us, it matters to him. Each day we must make some quick decisions, decisions that don't allow us to linger in prayer for wisdom. In times like that, remember the one-word prayer of the ages: "HELP!" Then go forward, making your choice quickly, and hold on confidently, knowing that God has blessed you with intellect—a brain for making choices—and he walks with you into the results of the decision.

Remember, too, that he promises to work for the good of those who love him (Romans 8:28). You can walk boldly into every situation and make God-pleasing choices, knowing and trusting that promise.

2. We allow God's Word to direct our decisions. Whenever we feast on Scripture, the Holy Spirit works in powerful ways. He desires that our taste buds of faith savor every ingredient of the divine recipe for life—whether we're taking our first bite or have been on a steady, daily diet of grace for years and years. The Spirit makes sure the flavor never fades. Opening the divine recipe book, we find the Holy Spirit's recipe for living. The psalmist puts it this way:

> *Your words are so choice, so tasty;*
> *I prefer them to the best home cooking.*
> *With your instruction, I understand life.*
>
> Psalm 119:103–104 THE MESSAGE

3. We copy the choices Jesus made while walking this earth. Observe how he responded to various situations. Reflect on the choices he made. Tap into his wisdom. Love like he loved—extravagantly—even loving those labeled "unlovable" by others. Seek out the Father's will, just as he did. The apostle Paul explains it this way:

> *Watch what God does, and then you do it,*
> *like children who learn proper behavior*
> *from their parents.*

Mostly what God does is love you.
Keep company with him and learn a life of love.
Observe how Christ loved us.
His love was not cautious but extravagant.
He didn't love in order to get something from us
but to give everything of himself to us.
Love like that.

Ephesians 5:1–2 THE MESSAGE

When we make choices based on Jesus' choices, we
show the Spirit is growing our faith-in-action. Instead
of worrying about the choices in front of us, we trust
the ways and will of God. That Spirit-created faith
changes the choices we make. It changes our living and
our loving. James writes this to us:

Dear friends,
do you think you'll get anywhere in this
if you learn all the right words but never do anything?
Does merely talking about faith
indicate that a person really has it?
For instance, you come upon an old friend dressed in rags
and half-starved and say,
"Good morning, friend! Be clothed in Christ!
Be filled with the Holy Spirit!" and walk off without
providing so much as a coat or a cup of soup—where does

that get you? Isn't it obvious that God-talk without
God-acts is outrageous nonsense?

James 2:14–17 THE MESSAGE

4. We keep on trusting God despite the difficulties and distractions Satan throws into the mix. A frustrated yet trusting prophet prayed these words. We can pray them, too. (Make sure to drink deeply from the encouragement found in the last four sentences.)

I'm overwhelmed with sorrow!
sunk in a swamp of despair!
I'm like someone who goes to the garden to pick cabbages
and carrots and corn and returns empty-handed,
finds nothing for soup or sandwich or salad.
There's not a decent person in sight.
Right-living humans are extinct.

But me, I'm not giving up.
I'm sticking around to see what GOD will do.
I'm waiting for God to make things right.
I'm counting on God to listen to me.

Micah 7:1–2, 7 THE MESSAGE

"Lettuce" Pray

Instead of throwing our hands in the air in despair, let us throw our prayers up to the one who makes us heirs of heaven. Stick around and see what God will do! He promises to not only listen to your prayers, but also to answer them.

5. We can have confidence in making choices, knowing that the God who created the universe and chose us as his own will help us make our smaller, everyday decisions, too. Just as Jesus chose his disciples, he has chosen us and brought us into his family:

> *You did not choose me, but I chose you*
> *and appointed you to go and bear fruit—*
> *fruit that will last.*
>
> *John 15:16 NIV*

God chose us as his own. He chose to create faith in us and give us the riches of heaven. He chose us to bear fruit—fruit that will last!

With all this in mind, you can choose the "let us" salad today:

- *Let us* realize that what we might consider insignificant choices aren't insignificant to God. If it matters to us, we can be assured it matters to him. And even when it doesn't matter to us, it matters to him.
- *Let us* allow God's Word to direct our decision process.
- *Let us* follow the example Jesus set for making choices while he walked this earth.
- *Let us* not become discouraged by the challenges and problems the world throws into the mix.
- *Let us* throw our prayers up to him who makes us heirs of heaven's riches instead of throwing our hands up in despair.
- *Let us* have confidence in making choices, knowing that since the God who created the universe chose us as his own, he will also work in us the wisdom to please him in our choices.

And *let us*
give thanks to the
Lord, our God,
for he
is good!

Taste and see!

I, your Lord, am good!

At the cross of Jesus
you'll see the truth . . .
up close and personal.

Taste tears of joy at his empty tomb,
now brimming with life.
Cry out—by day, by night:
"Touch me, Savior, and I will live!"
You will live!

Be prepared
for my life-changing touch.
Breathe in
the scent of grace and new life
through my Spirit.

Hear this, my child, whom I love:
your sins are forgiven.

Your senses are set free.
Free to serve me, as you serve others.

Touch, taste, smell, hear, and see that I am
and will always remain
your good and gracious Lord.

Tim Wesemann

I'm asking GOD for one thing,

only one thing:
To live with him in his house
my whole life long.
I'll contemplate his beauty;
I'll study at his feet.

Psalm 27:4 THE MESSAGE

Heavenly Broiled Fish (serves 4)

2 pounds skinned fish fillets (cod or other delicate white fish)
Fresh lemon

Sauce:
    1/2 cup grated parmesan
      1/4 cup soft butter
        3 tablespoons mayonnaise (not salad dressing)
        3 tablespoons chopped scallion tops
      1/4 teaspoon salt
      Dashes of Tabasco pepper sauce

RECIPE FOR LIFE
How sweet are your words to my taste. Psalm 119:103

Chicken and Potatoes

8 large drumsticks
(or 4 drumsticks, 4 thighs)
2 large potatoes, cut in wedges
1 onion, sliced
1 cup Roma tomatoes, cut up

1 teaspoon coarse salt
1/2 teaspoon pepper
4 teaspoons olive oil
Basil or oregano

Preheat oven to 350º. Lightly grease pan. Lay chicken in pan surrounded with potatoes. Place onion slices over chicken; pour tomatoes on top. Season with salt, pepper, oil, and basil. Cover pan with foil, and cook 25 minutes. Remove foil, turn chicken, baste, and cook 25 minutes without foil.

RECIPE FOR LIFE ♥
How sweet are your words to my taste. Psalm 119:103 NLT

Entrées

(Heavenly Broiled Fish, continued)

Preheat broiler 15 minutes. Mix together sauce ingredients. Place fillets on a greased, foil-lined jelly-roll pan. Squeeze lemon juice over fillets.

If fillets are thin, spread sauce over top and broil till golden.

If fillets are thick loins ($\frac{1}{2}$" or thicker), broil until half cooked, from top down to middle of fillet. Flip fillets over, and spread sauce over the uncooked side. Place back under broiler.

Broil until sauce turns golden brown. Sauce scorches easily; move oven rack down as needed.

Grilled Chicken Spread

½ cup mayonnaise
2 tablespoons Dijon mustard
1 tablespoon honey

Mix ingredients. Grill chicken until halfway cooked. Brush on spread. Continue grilling.

RECIPE FOR
How sweet are your words to my taste. ...3 NLT

THE ENTREE

KEEPING THE
MAIN THING
THE MAIN THING

The time has come for the main course. Our Host serves us. His eyes tell the story. How could so many emotions and thoughts fill one man's heart at one time? As he presents the main course, the window to his soul opens and we, so close, see in his eyes

- resolve, great resolve, as he "sets his face" toward Jerusalem and the cross that there awaits him (Luke 9:51);

- joy, even in enduring the cross, scorning its shame, and sitting at the right hand of the throne of God, so one day we can sit at his feet in heaven (Hebrews 12:2);

- great sadness as he weeps over Jerusalem and over those who missed out on the life-giving gifts he had for them (Luke 19:41–42);

- pain—sheer physical and emotional pain—like nothing we can imagine (John 19); and

- triumph as he recalls the victory over Satan and death he won for us, the guests at his table (1 Corinthians 15:51–55).

True Center-Peace

The main course, the center-peace, replicates the table's centerpiece—the message of the cross of Jesus Christ, our Savior! The cross and its message of salvation are the *meat* of God's Word. His cross stands front and center in our lives—a cross of sacrifice and redemption, a cross of wretchedness as well as triumph. Christ's cross looms boldly in the center of Scripture, with every truth—from Genesis to Revelation—finding its roots in that cross, in Christ crucified and Christ resurrected. Here we admire a true *center-peace*.

Never has the saying "The main thing is to keep the main thing the main thing" been more appropriate and applicable. The message of the cross must remain the "main thing" in our lives. And the main thing—the main ingredient—in our forgiven, abundant, and eternal lives is Jesus' death on the cross and subsequent resurrection. Yes, the main thing is to keep the main thing the main thing!

This focus on Christ and the redemption he earned for us makes absolutely no sense to those in the world who feed on cotton-candy spirituality. Human ideas of spiritual nutrition look nice and taste sweet, but deliver a lot of blown air instead of true substance. They provide no nutritional value, no strength for our souls.

Still, many in our world today try to survive on spiritual junk food, refusing to savor the true Gospel, the message of Christ's bloody cross and open tomb. Attitudes like this astonished the apostle Paul:

I am astonished that you are so quickly deserting him who called you in the grace of Christ and are turning to a different gospel—not that there is another one, but there are some who trouble you and want to distort the gospel of Christ. But even if we or an angel from heaven should preach to you a gospel contrary to the one we preached to you, let him be accursed.

Galatians 1:6–8

Foolish Junk Food

Paul also explains our sin-inspired appetite for spiritual junk food. How often we crave it, rather than the satisfying Good News of the Savior who holds the recipe for real life, true life, eternal life:

For the word of the cross is foolishness to those who are perishing, but to us who are being saved it is the power of God.

1 Corinthians 1:18 NASB

What an honor God gives by letting us share the main course with others, giving them a taste of the goodness and grace of God! What joy to see others respond as their spiritual taste buds come alive!

We may find ourselves distressed when others do not seem to keep the main thing the main thing. But we can't just point the finger at others. Why do *we* find it so easy to push ourselves away from the table as our Server brings the main course?

A close-up view of the "old rugged cross" brings us face-to-face with our sin and our need for the forgiveness our Savior won for us there. But don't we often prefer to keep that cross "on a hill far away," as the old hymn puts it? We may love the tune, but truth be told, the words make us dance:

> *I'm asking GOD for one thing,*
> *only one thing:*
> *To live with him in his house my whole life long.*
> *I'll contemplate his beauty;*
> *I'll study at his feet.*
>
> Psalm 27:4 THE MESSAGE

Our Savior-Host encourages us to make ourselves at home, in his home. As his friends and followers, we eat from his table. We sip from his cup of grace. We rejoice in his gifts of forgiveness and salvation won for us on the cross. We try—we really do try—to take it all in as we survey the gory, glorious cross of Jesus, who calls us to keep the main thing—the message of his cross—the main thing.

When I survey the wondrous cross
On which the Prince of glory died,
My richest gain I count but loss
And pour contempt on all my pride.

Forbid it, Lord, that I should boast
Save in the death of Christ, my God;
All the vain things that charm me most,
I sacrifice them to his blood.

See, from his head, his hands, his feet
Sorrow and love flow mingled down.
Did e'er such love and sorrow meet
Or thorns compose so rich a crown?

Were the whole realm of nature mine,
That were a tribute far too small;
Love so amazing, so divine,
Demands my soul, my life, my all!

Isaac Watts, 1674–1748

Why is everyone

hungry for more?
"More, more," they say.
"More, more."
I have God's more-than-enough,
More joy in one ordinary day
than they get
in all their shopping sprees.

Psalm 4:7 THE MESSAGE

Look at the birds

of the air;
they do not sow or reap
or store away in barns,
and yet your heavenly Father feeds them.
Are you not much more
valuable
than they?

Matthew 6:26 NIV

Do not labor

for the food that perishes,
but for the food that endures
to eternal life,
which the Son of Man will give to you.

Jesus said to them,
"I am the bread of life;
whoever comes to me shall not hunger, and
whoever believes in me
shall never thirst."

John 6:27, 35

Side Dish Recipes

Oven-Fried Potatoes

3 medium potatoes
¼ cup olive oil
1 tablespoon grated Parmesan
½ teaspoon salt
¼ teaspoon garlic powder

¼ teaspoon pepper
¼ teaspoon paprika (optional)

Scrub potatoes (do not peel). Cut into ⅛-inch round wedges. Place in baking pan, on end, slightly overlapping.

Combine remaining ingredients, stirring well. Brush potatoes with half of mixture.

RECIPE FOR LIFE
How sweet are your words to my taste. Psalm 11

(Oven-Fried Potatoes, continued)

Bake uncovered at 375° for 45 minutes, basting occasionally with remaining seasoned oil.

FLOUR

Green Bean Casserole

3–4 cans green beans
2 tablespoons butter
2 tablespoons flour
8 ounces sour cream

½ teaspoon salt
1 teaspoon sugar
Pepper
4 ounces shredded Swiss cheese

Melt butter; add flour and sour cream. Mix in salt, sugar, and pepper. Drain beans; add to mixture. Sprinkle cheese over top. Bake at 350º for 20–30 minutes.

RECIPE FOR LIFE

How sweet are your words to my taste. Psalm 119:103 NLT

Corn Casserole

16-ounce bag frozen corn
8 ounces cream cheese, softened
Pepper

Cook corn. Mix with cream cheese. Add pepper to taste.

RECIPE FOR LIFE

How sweet are your words to my taste.

SIDE DISHES

WHAT COMES WITH THE MAIN COURSE?

Do side dishes get a bad rap? They're on the *side!* When you ask someone to name their favorite food, it's usually an entrée, not a side dish like brussels sprouts! Are your side dishes in the early stages of developing an inferiority complex?

A four-year-old was asked to pray the blessing before Christmas dinner. Family members bowed their heads in expectation. He began his prayer, thanking God for all his friends, naming them one by one. Next he thanked God for Mommy, Daddy, Brother, Sister, Grandma, Grandpa, and all his aunts and uncles. Then he began to thank God for the turkey, the dressing, the fruit salad, the cranberry sauce, the pies, the cakes, even the whipped cream.

Then he paused, and everyone waited . . . and waited!

After a long silence, the young fellow looked up at his mother and asked, "If I thank God for the broccoli, won't he know I'm lying?"

Do "side dishes" come with the message of the cross?

They couldn't be served without the main course, but because of the message of the cross and empty tomb we also receive these "side dishes":

- A right relationship with God the Father!
- Heaven!
- Hope!
- Discernment!
- Confidence in and through Jesus!
- Humility!
- A servant's heart!
- Stability!
- Insights into God's Word!
- Contentment!
- Everyday strength!
- Healing—whether on earth or in heaven!
- Comfort!
- Christian friends!
- Calm in the midst of storms!
- Time and reasons to worship!
- A healthy appetite for God!
- Gratitude!
- Protection!
- Wisdom to know God's will!
- True joy!

What a menu!

The best news is that we don't have to choose, as in a restaurant, only two or three options. *All* belongs to us! All comes free with the main course—the message of the cross! Each complimentary side perfectly complements the message of Christ crucified!

Recall and rejoice in this promise from Jesus himself about his blessings:

> *But seek first the kingdom of God*
> *and his righteousness,*
> **and all these things will be added to you.**
>
> Matthew 6:33 (emphasis mine)

Please don't skim over the list on page 74.

Savor each plentiful morsel plentifully provided as a gift from our Savior. What a plateful of heavenly provisions! God is good and gracious—yes, all the time! Let your praises ascend, for the joy of the Lord is our strength (Nehemiah 8:10).

The Lord reminded me of his joy in those life-sustaining side dishes one day at a time when my family was planting a garden. Years ago, my wife and I would set aside one portion of our little garden for each of our three young children. The children would pick out what they would like to plant, care for the growing plants, and then watch God's miracle of life throughout the summer. In the fall they would reap the rewards of the vegetables or fruits they had tended.

When we asked our son Benjamin what he would like to plant in his vegetable (side dish) garden, he quickly replied, "Mashed potatoes!"

The boring, practical, no-fun adult in us felt the temptation quickly to respond, "No! You can't do that. Pick something else." But his answer instead became a great joy-filled lesson in finding nourishment in God's side dishes! Why squelch a fun and creative idea? Mashed potatoes? Why not! So what if the neighbors see us! Let's even make a little marker that reads "Mashed Potatoes" to mark the spot in the fertile ground. Let's praise the Lord with a garden complete with a bumper crop of mashed potatoes. And maybe, while we're at it, we should add some chocolate ice-cream plants! Praise the Lord with chocolate! *(And all of God's chocolate lovers said, "Amen!")*

Bloom Where You're Planted!

I love considering God's joy when he did some planting of his own:

- Who would have thought that something great could come out of the little town of Bethlehem? But the Holy Spirit planted baby Jesus in Mary's womb and, after nine months, the world's Savior was born!

- Imagine the surprise of the early Christians when Jesus decided to plant a persecutor, a murderer (!), Saul, in his garden to bear fruit.

Ever wonder why your Lord decided to plant you where you are? Don't underestimate God or his ability to work miracles through the power of his Word of forgiveness and life at work through your words.

Go ahead! Praise him right now for causing faith to grow in what you might once have considered your own unproductive garden! Let these words from the inspired writer James encourage your hungry and fertile heart:

> *In simple humility, let our gardener,*
> *God, landscape you with the Word,*
> *making a salvation-garden of your life.*
>
> James 1:21 THE MESSAGE

God picks every one of his side dishes from the salvation garden planted and growing at the cross and outside the garden tomb of his Son, our Savior, Jesus Christ. Every ingredient needed for his recipe for life grows in this fertile soil.

Go ahead—dive into our Savior's life-giving side dishes! The recipes taste divine and—well, let's just say, Jesus thinks you're to die for!

Make a joyful noise

to the LORD, all the earth! Serve the LORD
with gladness! Come into his presence with
singing! Know that the LORD, he is God!
It is he who made us, and we are his;
we are his people,
and the sheep of his pasture.
Enter his gates with thanksgiving,
and his courts with praise!
Give thanks to him; bless his name!
For the LORD is good;
his steadfast love endures forever,
and his faithfulness to all generations.

Psalm 100

Blessed is everyone

who fears the LORD,
who walks in his ways!
You shall eat the fruit
of the labor of your hands;
you shall be blessed,
and it shall be well with you.

Psalm 128:1–2

The LORD bless you

and keep you;
the LORD make his face to shine upon you
and be gracious to you;
the LORD lift up his countenance upon you
and give you peace.

Numbers 6:24–26

Peach Dumpling *(serves 4)*

Pastry for 1 deep-dish pie
Sugar

4 large peaches, washed and dried
(not pitted; peeled or unpeeled)

Preheat oven to 350º.
Sprinkle each peach with sugar just before encasing in crust.
Divide piecrust into four equal parts. Wrap each piece around a peach, encasing the peach completely.
Use any scraps of dough to form leaves and stems.
Attach leaves by brushing dough with water.

RECIPE FOR LIFE ♥
How sweet are your words to my taste. Psalm 119:103 NLT

(Peach Dumpling, continued)

Place in an ungreased, nonstick 9x13-inch pan, or use a muffin tin to avoid losing juice. Bake 45 minutes or until crust is brown.

Peach Dumpling Sauce:
½ cup butter
1 teaspoon almond extract

1 ½ cups powdered sugar
1 egg, beaten

While peaches are baking, melt butter over low heat in a small saucepan. Remove from heat. Whisk in powdered sugar and almond extract. Gradually whisk in egg. Return to medium-low heat. Cook, stirring constantly, until mixture bubbles. Spoon sauce over hot peach dumplings.

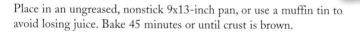

Dessert Rec

Strawberry Ribbon Pie

1 10-inch deep-dish graham-cracker crust
1 3-ounce package strawberry Jell-O
¼ cup sugar
¾ cup boiling water
2 cups frozen strawberries with ¼ cup sugar added

2 teaspoons lemon juice
½ package (4 ounces) cream cheese, softened
1 teaspoon vanilla
2 cups whipped topping

Pour boiling water over Jell-O and sugar, stirring to dissolve. Add sweetened strawberries, and crush lightly as they soften.

RECIPE FOR LIFE 💗
How sweet are your words to my taste. Psalm 119:103 NLT

(Strawberry Ribbon Pie, continued)

Add lemon juice. Cool until mixture mounds slightly.

Beat vanilla into softened cream cheese. Gradually add the whipped topping.

Spread half of the cream-cheese mixture into the graham-cracker crust. Spoon half of the fruit mixture over the cream-cheese layer. Chill 20–30 minutes. Repeat with another layer each of cream cheese and strawberries.

Chill at least 3 hours.

This dessert is equally good with raspberries.

DESSERTS

SWEET BLESSINGS!

While we wait for the desserts to arrive, let's take a moment to reflect on where this meal began—back to the preparations. John 10:10 describes these preparations in the words of our Savior:

> *I came that they may have life and have it abundantly.*

Eugene Peterson translates the same verse this way in THE MESSAGE:

> *[Jesus said,] "I came so they can have real and eternal life, more and better life than they ever dreamed of."*

Jesus came to earth specifically to prepare a banquet, a life of salvation blessings for us, a lifetime of blessings, first here on earth and then unending blessings in his eternal, heavenly banquet hall.

The desserts that top off this banquet of life encompass all the sweet blessings we receive from the hand of our Lord.

Sweet Indulgence

Some people don't care for desserts and others avoid them due to health or dietary restrictions, but no one needs to turn away from the sweet blessings that Jesus serves!

Go ahead! Indulge yourself! There's no need to wait for a special occasion. Our generous Host makes the sweet blessings of life available every hour of every day. He doesn't hide them in the pantry or reserve them only for consumption on Sunday morning or Wednesday evening.

Think about it this way: We've tasted the goodness of our Lord in his sacrificial, life-giving, sin-cleansing death and resurrection. We've savored the peace of mind and heart that comes with the message of the cross and empty tomb. And the cherry on top, so to speak, includes generous helpings of sweet blessings that God serves up throughout our days. You know the ones. Sweet blessings such as

- friends who pray for you daily, especially when Satan preys on you;
- a baby's coo and, well, *almost* anything they do;
- dishwashers, and having the dishes that need washing;
- teachers and principals and teachers with principles;

- a hand to hold for better or worse;
- a sale on shoes as well as shoes that aren't on sale;
- extended time without a virus—in your body or on your computer;
- scrapbooks and books you can't bear to scrap;
- those who encourage you when you're discouraged;
- friends named *Grace,* and friends who live out the true meaning of grace;
- enjoying dessert with a friend, and knowing that friend won't desert you!

The list of God's sweet blessings could continue for pages on end. Our generous Lord offers us extravagant, sweet blessings to sustain us on our daily walk with him through life. Let there be no doubt about it:

> *[We're] blessed when [we've] worked up a good appetite for God. He's food and drink in the best meal [we'll] ever eat.*
>
> Matthew 5:6 THE MESSAGE

Has the offer of heaven's sweet blessings stirred up in your heart an attitude of thankfulness to God? I hope so, because you now have the opportunity to help complete this *dessert* section of the recipes for life! On the following pages you'll find room to write, reflect, and send your compliments to the Chef, who prepared it all especially for you!

Sweet blessings I received from Jesus in my growing-up years:

RECIPE FOR LIFE 💜
How sweet are your words to my taste. Psalm 119:103 NLT

Sweet blessings I've received from Jesus as a grown-up:

RECIPE FOR LIFE 💜
How sweet are your words to my taste. Psalm 119:103 NLT

Sweet blessings I've received from Jesus for my faith life:

RECIPE FOR LIFE 🖤
How sweet are your words to my taste. Psalm 119:103 NLT

**Sweet blessings I look forward to receiving,
trusting his perfect love and flawless timing:**

RECIPE FOR LIFE 🖤
How sweet are your words to my taste. Psalm 119:103 NLT

Feed your children,
God most holy,
Comfort sinners poor and lowly;
You our Bread of Life
from heaven,
Bless the food you here
have given!
As these gifts the body nourish,
May our souls in graces flourish
Till with saints in
heav'nly splendor
At your feast our thanks
we render.
Amen.

Johann Heermann, 1585–1647

After-Dinner Mints

4 tablespoons water
1 cup granulated sugar
1 cup powdered sugar
Peppermint extract, to taste
Food coloring
Waxed paper

Spread out waxed paper on which to cool mints.

Bring the mixture of granulated sugar and water to a boil.

RECIPE FOR LIFE ♥

How sweet are your words to my taste. *Psalm 119:103 NLT*

(After-Dinner Mints, continued)

Mix in peppermint extract, food coloring, and powdered sugar. Let mixture cool to thicken slightly.

Quickly drop spoonfuls of the mixture onto the waxed paper. Form into any shape you desire—even the shape of a cross!

AFTER-DINNER MUSIC

AND A MINT

Our Host serves an after-dinner mint as we relax by his side. Normally, an after-dinner mint cleanses the diners' palates. But we certainly don't want to remove our Savior's grace from the taste buds of our faith! Rather, for us this mint only enhances the other courses prepared from our Lord's recipes for life:

> *Your words are so choice, so tasty;*
> *I prefer them to the best home cooking.*
> *With your instruction, I understand life.*
>
> Psalm 119:103–104 THE MESSAGE

As you linger over the sweetness of this "mint," what choice, tasty words of God come to mind? What promises? What assurances? What hope?

> *I will never leave you nor forsake you.*
>
> Hebrews 13:5

> *Cast . . . all your anxieties on him,*
> *because he cares for you.*
>
> 1 Peter 5:7

> *It is God who works in you, both to*
> *will and to work for his good pleasure.*
>
> Philippians 2:13

[Jesus said,] "I have called you friends."

John 15:15

May the God of peace himself sanctify you completely, and may your whole spirit and soul and body be kept blameless at the coming of our Lord Jesus Christ.

1 Thessalonians 5:23

Music with Your Mint?

Elegant (and not-so-elegant) restaurants pipe in music for diners to enjoy. Music enhances enjoyment. As you think about offering a musical gift to your Host after dinner, does an appropriate hymn or praise chorus come to mind?

As you consider that, realize you're not the only one providing after-dinner music. Your heavenly Father also sings; he sings a song of joy over you! Don't believe me? You have *his* Word on it!

The LORD your God is with you,
he is mighty to save.
He will take great delight in you,
he will quiet you with his love,
he will rejoice over you with singing.

Zephaniah 3:17 NIV

Yes, you read that last line correctly. The Lord rejoices over you with singing! (Are you quickly scanning the dinner table, searching for the humble pie? What humbling words!)

Ask yourself, "Who am I that the Lord chooses to sing over me?!" This same Jesus loved spending time with sinners while he walked Israel's dusty paths:

> *Now the tax collectors and sinners were*
> *all drawing near to hear him. And the Pharisees and*
> *the scribes grumbled, saying,*
> *"This man receives sinners and eats with them."*
>
> *Luke 15:1–2*

Jesus loved eating with those who knew their spiritual poverty, those who felt spiritual hunger pangs. He loved assuring them of his full forgiveness and giving them new life, a whole new wardrobe. After meeting Jesus and coming into a faith relationship with him, they wore only the "Robes of Righteousness" label. That label read "Made with love, by hand—actually two hands—nailed to a cross." Jesus also loves to keep company with us—sinners all, no doubt! He loves to welcome us into his home, to eat with us and sing over us!

Come, taste, see, *and listen,* for the Lord is good! And that infinite goodness causes us to break out in songs of praise to him in response. Sing, and sing some more! Rejoice and sing . . . Jesus did, and he still does! He takes great delight in you. He rejoices over you with singing!

Two After-Dinner Music Suggestions

Praise God, from whom all blessings flow;
Praise him, all creatures here below;
Praise him above, ye heav'nly host:
Praise Father, Son, and Holy Ghost.
Amen!

Thomas Ken, 1637–1711

I am Jesus' little lamb,
Ever glad at heart I am;
For my Shepherd gently guides me,
Knows my need and well provides me,
Loves me ev'ry day the same,
Even calls me by my name.

Day by day, at home, away,
Jesus is my staff and stay.
When I hunger, Jesus feeds me,
Into pleasant pastures leads me;
When I thirst, he bids me go
Where the quiet waters flow.

Who so happy as I am,
Even now the Shepherd's lamb?
And when my short life is ended,
By his angel host attended,
He shall fold me to his breast,
There within his arms to rest.

Henrietta von Hayn, 1724–82